HIGHWAY TO THE SKY

A Frank O'Hara Award Book

MICHAEL BROWNSTEIN

HIGHWAY TO THE SKY

Published for the Frank O'Hara Foundation

at Columbia University Press, New York & London

1969

Some of these poems first appeared in the following publications: *The Paris Review, The Floating Bear, C, The Yale Literary Magazine, Angel Hair, Juillard, Ronald Reagan, Spice, The World, Best and Company, Adventures in Poetry*, and in the anthologies, *The Young American Poets*, Follett, 1968 and *An Anthology of New York Poets*, Random House, 1969.

THE 1969 FRANK O'HARA AWARD FOR POETRY

The annual Frank O'Hara Award for Poetry, named for the American poet who was killed in 1966, was established by the Frank O'Hara Foundation to encourage the writing of experimental poetry and to aid in its publication. The award is meant to carry on in some measure Frank O'Hara's interest in helping new poets in their work. Eligible for it are poets who have not had a book of poetry published or accepted for publication by a commercial or university press. Further information about the award is available from the Frank O'Hara Foundation at Columbia University Press, which published in 1968 the first Frank O'Hara Award Book, *Spring in This World of Poor Mutts,* by Joseph Ceravolo.

Michael Brownstein is the winner of the 1969 Frank O'Hara Award for Poetry. Born in Philadelphia in 1943, he grew up in New Jersey, Tennessee, and Ohio and studied at Antioch College and the New School in New York City. He has lived on the West Coast and for a year in Europe, where he studied and translated French poetry under a Fulbright grant. His work has appeared in many magazines, and a collection of his poetry has been privately printed: *Behind the Wheel,* C Editions, 1967. Michael Brownstein now lives in New York City.

The design for the jacket of the clothbound edition and the cover of the paperbound edition of this book is by Joe Brainard.

CONTENTS

HIGHWAY TO THE SKY

CHILDREN, IT'S TIME

The day I was born
The birds stopped singing

The day I was born
The birds started singing

Take your pick
While I take mine

NATIONS

In the history of the nations
There is a great reserve
Of the other nations. All of us
Live on the table of silence, like Spaniards.
Other nations, for the noisy
As well. Spain and silence
Of this all-wide-awake world
Silence each other: that is why we can draw
Our human being generations
From time to time flow
In a hard line to the noise
Of the next, sometimes interrupted by an age
And fill it with some girls and chairs.

Noise and general loudness contribute
To omens: the silent flight of wooden birds
The inward figurations of Mobile
And nature could easily relax into the human world
Whole nations spilling in the loud places
Of history, Martin and Diane starting
To unravel again. Diane, tell your mother
Nations are the mahogany of the great reserve
Spain, South, Siam
Little tables around the world.

I AM NOT THE CONSTANT READER

Do you read
Yes, and it is a form of life
So long as I forget what's that I'm reading

Yet gradually not to read at all, you respond
Is when you get up enough for roll call

But I do not believe in roll call
Although I see it
Through a round window flanked by plants
In China long ago

*

She has no need for old men
To water her plants   They are asked to dismiss
Themselves from the service and wander disconsolate
Like a broken radio ejected from the filling station
Serving northern Quebec

*

The men and women inhabiting northern Quebec
Speak a brand of French poorly burnt
Into the hide   They read very little, but constantly
Like the British mouldering on a protectorate

This particular British is grading papers
Sent to him from far across the sea
Concerning life in an attempted passage
From ancient history

WOMAN WALKING SLOWLY DOWNSTAIRS AND WAVING

I am a nation, and smother the crusted cloud
is a larger nation, an army of sleep
an even larger one, the pillow and hair
wave of information theory, putting me to bed
or if not to bed, to dream
of unscheduled planes, dozing in their hulking syndrome
one turbine only perhaps awake, and that is me
the honeybee, and that is you
sighing for a separation between the two

4

PANATELLA

In the rafter morning under the rafters
The Sun seen as Hand opens a trunk
A vicious or kindly old man he beats back
The band swaddling tight blond pleats
On this some-how furrowed land of hair. Otherwise
Known as air . . . "Oh, I know,
I belittle the staggering reach of your intellect
In order to cross over quicker," he said
To himself, "to the other side, there
I can beach my canoe and fabricate something
To explain my never having used a paddle."
The sun said this in a skit. Cold swift trucks
Were balling past outside, they could be heard
In the United States of America.
"Oh, yes," snort the truck drivers,
"We are the teamsters of the United States
of America." The Sun said this in a skit.

STEPPING OUT

A tile is loose for splendid feet
Of cognition running with arms outspread.
An airman who treasures the small silver wings pinned
At his shoulder by a functionary so he can take off
Without necessarily a clear conscious, but an ordered
One, a veritable flying bridge.

If the tile is loose, throw it away

Suddenly Syria: midday: telegrams call
In the upper air, as a muezzin drones from a mosque
Or that muezzin drones from that mosque
Just to the left, and you forget your bags,
Transfixed.

Transfixed and
Gone, like an artichoke Louisiana has peeled.
She has eaten. She gathers the great purple folds
Of her mammy dress together and with a purposeful sigh,
Strides off. "Not enough commas in this poem," she mutters.
That may be true, there aren't many pauses in the poem
Of life, but just like her to say so, she
being illiterate mammy.
And bearing her simple grudge she gains upon the distance.

If the tile is truly loose, drop it in your pocket

Or paste it back in its pattern
On the floor of the mosque. Quick, before
The murderous Arabs see you. They see you: it is too late?

The cool delicious floor your feet touch
Stepping out of the midday heat (midday again?)
With the rest of your body, not at all a coming-out party,
But a soothing and honest rest on the actual precious stones.

LIFE

Life is beautiful.   However

The only truly human, American expressions
                    of its staggering rich moments
            (two baby bulldogs in open window, 3:17 A.M.)
Aren't really forms of expression like language, but

The only truly human, American expressions
                    of its staggering rich moments
            (two baby tomatoes in open window, 3:17 A.M.)
Aren't really forms of expression like language, but

Parallels manifesting themselves right alongside
Those moments, like music. It is just
Your specific choice in music, the one when you respond,
Dropping onto my back as I walk past
                    flinging Tasty Cake . . .
Your breasts that have chosen their call, for always
        they drift ahead of what you plan on leaving
            in your mind and its musical chair.

Genius, to eat and mumble in peace . . .

So, the definition of tragedy is
"A waste of time that you stop to consider it"
And not stop to consider this: applying
Force to the mirror which by itself
Already is falling away from self-consciousness,
Nemesis of the 20th century . . . to do that
Would be a waste of time. Or would it?
Making the right choice is calm laughter
      when it occurs to you except as an idea.

I say "American" because the universe, all the radar
Technicians of enticement, is American now
Entirely. I say "nineteen" because
Nineteen is your age, and take
Your life into my hands
And you take mine, we jump into the truth.

SKETCHES FROM NATURE

. . . Mellow silence, peaceful prairie dream, sandwich
      soaking in the stream.

The deer and elves now make their run
  across wintry midnight carpets . . .
the wind, too, makes its—says

Nature nutritive, sportsmen crass . . .
    like a baby-minded mother at a double bass
who pauses in rapture at the gut of the bow, a rapture
     such as adolescent gourmets know, and love
to know, and know they love this. This they know:
    a cup of raspberries drowned in cream, glittering sundae
of mountain valley far below, yoked and snorting
     palomino by the quivering stream, mind at peace
and heart at ease, and limbs and hair and heart in dream.

Wake up, the mountain gentian's bell in pungent toil . . .

Wake up! A weird and in fact unique butterfly
has already disappeared, I was awake and saw it,
        and said to it, "Stay, until my friend awakes:
do not go, or no one else shall know"

His cactus buttons dropped along the desert floor
                to mark the way he was thirsting for . . .

Two walrus, quite eerie
three more appear in total stillness
of an uninhabited Oregon coast at dusk.
A naturalist witnessing the scene begins to weep
for joy. A small child of either sex joins him:
                it's a tableau, simple and real.
        No "symbols," no straining after a meaning
that wasn't there in the beginning, obvious to all,
                before the first walrus appeared . . .

Sunflower, fat with summer
        stirs beside a willow tree, whose tips
touch a block of butter flung into the pond:
                        it floats! It looks just like the sun!

EVOLUTION

Today the gently curving claw
A bird lights up on my shoulder—
Having no need to remember
Wings flapping
I am anywhere above the ground

In this way the eyeball also glows

I don't need to remember eyeballs roll
Or even that they roll
Up against something that
Is not rolling
That is called abstraction
If I were you and I guess I am
I would dispense with it
Like a tin soldier you have been opening

Bright cans marked FOOD until
I hand you this pass

There is no need to look at it
Unless you look away

Tortoise shells cigarettes fingerprints

Tortoise-shell comb
Tragic cigarette
Upper fingerprint

Awake on the face
The river flows and no one knows

Warm in the morning if you wish
Cool afternoons
Genius under the lamp through the night

SOME DEFINITIONS

a noise: a band of musicians

pass not: care not

savor: understanding

waving: waiving

to: compared to

began: began to say

imp: engraft feathers in a damaged wing

prove: experience to the full

farmers: cultivators of land they do not own

mere: absolute

remorse: pity

the self: language here fails as mathematics has before it

can: is skilled in

determined: ended

crazy tempers: delicate constitutions

preferred: promoted

adamant: one who dispenses with clothes

the second: lip to lip being the first, lip to
                           heart, through the ear, is the second

commence: graduate

grace: too-clever riders are not good at horseplay

bait: food on a journey

center: center of the Earth

teeming: the full moon

curious: pineapples

needless: having no wants, quite content

amber: the power of slowly moving jaws

whets: exquisite

climactic: critical, marking an epoch

perspective: and into Glory peep

YESTERDAY

Yesterday, after the day's workness, I walked down
past the canals and houses to the shore of our river.
Pausing alongside a fragrant pair of young trees I gave
myself away to great-breeze thoughts, the nature and
subtleties of our people and its long studded history,
a history swelled with stories that reach back to the
earliest days, the days of the Cloud.

I passed many stories through my mind and
passed my emotions through the stories, slowly weaving
with half-closed eyes the tapestry-without-a-
proper-name. Finally my temples pulsed with delight
and throbbed with recognition: I had reached the Cloud.

"Cloud," I whispered hoarsely, "words almost
fail me before a cloud, but I want to understand: why
does it rain all the time? What's the idea? What can
I substitute for all these histories, I get so tired weaving
this rug and meanwhile it's pouring on my head,
you know? My brain always turns into a rain forest."

"That's beautiful," the Cloud replied. "The rain forest,
that's beautiful. You don't appreciate that if you really
were to leave here headed for the desert, you could only bring
along some ass to carry your supplies. If it's not the rain,
the ultraviolet rays will get you. Buy an umbrella!
Umbrellas are more than they seem, in fact they lie, open,
at the heart of every problem, except the last one,
maybe . . . But I wouldn't become obsessed with that, because
you don't actually know if it's anything more than the word
'problem' yet. Just keep working away on
your carpet, it's very fine, and when the cloud
design envelops the rest I may even buy it from you . . .
I really like clouds."

"But all that's just talk," I protested, leaning forward as the
Cloud began to thin out, "although it's been amazing enough."

"What were you expecting me to say?" the Cloud
hissed. "If you really want to know, the way I see it,
it's all visible. OK?"

"All visible? But I had to close my eyes to talk to you,"
I said, opening my eyes and seeing bends in the river,
then one bend, then sheen on water . . .
A large craft was approaching across the sheen, but
hogging the glare so most of it was bleached out. It looked like
what's called a hovercraft, though until then I had only
seen pictures of hovercrafts. A sizable crowd
was aboard and already I recognized a few faces, people,
some others. I saw them, and instantly joy coupling
with boredom rolled across my face. But that's another story,
we began weaving it today two or three minutes
after the boat touched shore.

LILY FLOWER

Lily flower
The telephone is ringing but you do not hear it
Because you are different
You have your own telephone

WAITRESS

Waitress
You bring my food, I give you money
I am full of food now and ready to go
But you still have to wait

WAR

You can't spend all day staring into the sea, however
As if it were your favorite book
Until an especially coddled page detaches itself
From the light, floating toward you through the grove
At the edge of which Hernando stands with the battalion
Bent to the amplification of his will, louder
And louder as it hums among the spindles
Of the fruit and garden trees. You *can*
Spend the day clearing out the porch and
Cease staring into that sea because it is
An unenlightening sea, furtively complex like an icy bath
With the washrag salesman's daughter. Laughter.
Wind ruffling the skirts of the citrus trees.
Soldiers are whining to seal off this port.
                    Oppose these soldiers.
Ignore them if they take your picture off
The wall . . . They take your picture from the wall
And walk through. You however are eating a pear
And don't need to see them down the rest
Of the hall to the door, out into the street
And crabbing, disappear into a fault. A busy town goes up.
You are not a traffic signal. But as it changes
A cop revolves, seriously intent on detaining you.
He doesn't care about the traffic, adding up behind you
Like a stifled thought, because he is whispering
Softly near your ear. The sun sinks along
His nightstick, all things relaxing into silence
Except for that stifled thought.

AROUND THE MOUTH

When love turns to hate as it does sometimes
You will find a specific reason
Because thought really is twined into the body
And looking at only one reason, of whatever kind
Distorts what has happened, such a conclusion
Too simple to be true, is probably true
Because actually many connecting rooms for your love
And why it disappeared exist, or don't disappear
In the city you and I were building under
Meditation's distant guns
                          But hate, not to mention love
Shouts at you what it means, and is so indistinct
In fact telling you something different,
You remember, when it was love
And nothing else, lifting through the blinds of
A motel instead of not lifting through the blinds
Of a motel or wherever   You were there
Maybe because a car gets tired like a horse
But I doubt it   I don't hate you but I doubt it
And like a rock- and bottle-throwing flare-up
Los Angeles intrudes upon the mind and
Trees near the sea become bored
                          with the ill at ease
While if you're at ease for a long period, not forever
You feel and even look beautiful
Although being at ease is not love

POEM

An evening's light rain and you start to smile

SPIRAL LANDSCAPE

Suddenly I was in the act of soaping my head
At the public bath Paris rue St. Antoine
When from behind me a door no doubt slammed
Into noises of other people (the sundry people)
With just as much right to live as me
On the edge of achieving their cleanliness

While then and there a plan came into view—
We're all to rise up and multiply to choke
In a manner of speaking entire worlds of strife
A perspective of cleanliness inside the nut
A door slammed enough to shake the Foundation
The research chemists & their assistants dropped
Their tubes instantly trailing lab coats lather talent
And in one pleasing swarm descended the stairs to
Exit and collect aimlessly in the great greens
A towering gardener sketches on his knees

Without the right to breathe exactly like me

But now I had a clan in mind—
For clean as a thistle the lab men yet grow slack
And wheeze a day behind the news like pioneers
Words that die into a ravenous ear, tying up
Surprise in a greasy phial of consternation

At that a giant clam surfaced in my thought
It therefore also monopolized my life and forced me
Out of the now dank clammy water and after dryness
To exit and the sunny street and I no longer walk alone
Though I'm moving in a unique position

Now I cross the human face

All this would be in living color
To satisfy your sight until you move

JUMPING

Inside the closing fist
of logical positivism a girl
and her chaperone are playing ping
pong until the balls just drop.
It's the touchy procrastination of human energy, not
a healthy situation . . . You take lunch
in a double wicker basket, over the hill
into a palm-shaped clearing
and spread a red checked tablecloth.
You smooth it over the hedge, dills,
tuna, beer and snow. The snow ants
meet the red ants and tussle
on red checks and in the sunbeams.
You watch them separately converge
from nowhere slowly, almost basking themselves
until they fall on each other at random
in sparkling flurries.

THEY

They don't disturb your sleep
   They don't disturb your day

BABY JESUS AND THE RHINESTONES

"The important thing to remember is that everyone
actually is a genius . . ." I am mentioning the word "genius" so
often now because this morning I discovered that I
hadn't thought or spoken that word in more than
eight months. It is absolutely necessary to keep all things
as balanced as possible: Someday perhaps we'll
sit down and have a talk about silence.

THWHALE

When I was six no eleven years old something . . . I
spotted a swollen whale stranded on the beach and we
went down to it to see it. Whale. Vast. Dead.
The mouth partly open; I remember a fine, painfully sunburned
girl wearing a faded bathing suit climbed to the teeth
and touched them. Then shit, she disappeared!

Pretty soon other beachside people were climbing the
whale, as they called it. The tail was in the sea. Down at
Entropy Beach—although actually I came up with that name just
now, after all these years . . . Then it was called Ocean Beach,
or Blue Woodside Beach, but it was really just the beach.
The whale was maybe ninety feet long, twenty feet
high, humped above closed eyes. I recall running my hand
along its rough canvas skin-covering, then its big eye
jumped open and said, "Thwale!" God . . . until I realized it
was just the lifeguard standing next to me who had said
that. And sure enough, when I turned to say
"What?" to him, the eye closed. For good I presume,
because then I was climbing the whale too.

It was a hulking pink and white whale dead on the beach
but not smelling yet that we spotted late in the afternoon,
the day after a violent rainstorm during which I saw a man
shafted by a thunderbolt as he shinnied up a flagpole
to retrieve the American flag.

31

THE CIRCUS

Yes, the circus has finally come to town! Ned and
his pet monkey, Julian, moonlight as umpires at the local
ball park, trained seals during the week at the zoo . . .
What to do about this: Ned needs increasing amounts of
money as the months pass to support the array of expensive,
debilitating habits that spell constant grief for his
folks. But Ned is lazy, the monkey has to do it all.
Julian is farmed out around the clock to support these
costly habits (heroine, booze, commercial television,
introspection, apathy, cynicism, etc.). So Julian labors
constantly. He is the pet monkey you see in all those
subway advertisements and in the movies, he's also the
unhappy one you've seen strapped to a behavioral psychologist's
chair and covered with electrodes, as well as most
of the other monkeys in public places. "The idea is to
launch the monkey into outer space for over 30 days, to test
the effect of zero gravity on his well-being," blares
your radio. Julian as ultimate monkey, docile archetype
of all monkeys, now playing at Universal Showcase Theatres
all over town! But Julian is sad; at night, while the rest
of the world sleeps, the circus beckons him. Deep within
he hears the call of the three rings he remembers so well.
The horses and prancing sequined girls, the lions and their
hungry tamers, the ringmaster happily cracking his whip.
Tightrope walkers, holidays on air, the glittering trapeze
artists holding their breath as they let go and sail
into the sky.

METABOLISM

Yours the taught climb borne security
Hop the store where quite sure sense is bought
From home, like children on a litmus, bathing.
You're clean and white, what is all this called? It is
Called a star. Then what is comfort to aged sister
Star? You win. A scissor wind, night wale,
Full arch sea, full for such good measure of
Diversity. The pain of sister sunlight,
The pleasure, sister water flap
Over tail light star. You are the bonus
Anonymous, baby like oven, love like balmy
Genius. Sail past where self is served
To self, as star to star receding in your area.
Chemist, baker, cellar, you all know
Calibrate the self and tamper momma
Cooling the heel as some lost star
Collides in separate peace: you are.

BEHIND THE WHEEL

Deep well corporals ride alongside listen
and ride   Small fork motions
for the magazine shell
pink developing Guadalupe under young
springing off the board to feel
the warm systems   Erased the second time
you remember her strong intelligent hands
as they passed the verge of speaking to you

Careens off the bore

We are now ready set squat
lips wearing a shoreline resolve to
talk again in laps   oil and sand blue
from hard riding   Chiefs weighted
some of the more plausible contours
her bookish ass ascends   "yes my daughter
very beautiful bare-legged and brown"
breasts brimming over into listen
and talk   On and off   a big Latin band
moistens its reeds and leaves backstage
"very beautiful   thirty silver blankets
around thirty silver minds"   That fits so close
rain pours from the manuscript

                    Clears up
A few extreme fine clouds   The sun
is rising along the alveolar ridge
like trying to establish in a valley the exact line
separating the two hills on either side
And then establishing it   it thrives
it works   you roll down the window
the girl parachutes onto the plain

SOMETHING ELSE

Here are three students
in the shade
a boy and two girls
studying French.
A plane drones.
One of the girls picks herself up
walks across the grass
behind her dormitory
in the sunlight. . . . . . .
To her dormitory.

The other two continue reading

Students teachers and gardeners
cross the field in small
loose figures, some talking
at various times
or alone—
to a class or workroom
or to eat something
or take a nap

It's twenty of three
in 1951
I am 8 years old
and somewhere else

When I am 18 I will be here

(When I am 28 I will be many)

BIG CITY

As I walk down NYC I wonder into the ground
Glee a short road across my face
To a sparrow observing from the cool agenda
Of the wind in the breeze . . . Not to fox this into
Something you just won't be able to grip
On your way downtown into work. "Let it be clear and distinct
Like the shoulder a French cook knows will serve four."

Knows might serve for

Always uncertain as to who will surface from the tube
Gripping a bath towel for me too. Which I wouldn't throw in
To your perfervid poet's face because you won't be a poet
Or a painter a spidery preacheress or candlestick maker
Though actually I can see you as the last.   For like the sky
I have no physical third eye,   psychically
Beside the point and valid as music: Now.

Do pigeons ever get headaches
Pecking as they do at the hard cement
Which is really a sidewalk? This and a dozen others
The sweatered infant asks. He is precocious of course
And steps on your stone. You offer him a palm and now
He's yowling, and his mother isn't girl anymore
Idly paused for limousine on green-leaved street.
Do you lean toward the girl?   Such is the tragedy by
Ugly inference of urban motherhood.

But we are all young mothers though only some show it
Barely struck by the hammer of joy.
A truck robs the eye of cobbles
But you could be looking at the truck
And keep looking, until big letters appear on one side

TYPHOON

Some carpenters gruff on the next roof
I see three from here but I was out earlier
Visiting and talk with a friend I reached
Those carpenters gone now
Everything outside quiet light
Including my sunglasses

Ripping up the surface tar
Because a month before (February 4th) a person
A fire partly burn it   I grew more

A Pontiac passed a wide row
House plants under the rear seat window
I see three from here

NAVEL

Sunkist
A fault shows up in the town
Bending with a jump or two over to the river
In it the fellows appear, seeing colors
Forwarded through their busy staffs
Hallowed out at the center

The river is blue
The buildings, in various stages of conduction
Into it the fellows fit the flowers
To be resembled later on one long stem

A sudden person wearing shorts (open short sleeves)
Drops it in the shade
On one stem near the book lowered onto
                          the beachhead
On one stem near the orange lowered
                          into the forehead

LOST IN A CORRIDOR OF POWER

The growth of raw power brings you to one knee
Like the Prince (any of our people) before Snow White

Before snow white the beavers pause
Their dish of prunes
Petroleum-colored beside them

The them
And the us go off
To play   Explosions   Polite Applause

"I'm going to watch here a few minutes then
when there's a slight pause unconscious
like a pause for breath I'll slowly TIP
onto the glass floor dozens of brass pans
and kettles all this crockery I have
in young cardboard box ready & waiting"

                    SMASH*

If that were on a tape recorder (and it is),
I know you would hear an infinitesimal sort of
Highly charged hush in the pause
Just split second before the smash hit

It would manifest as a slight suction, drop in pressure:

SUCK   SUCK   *

                     *SMASH***

That hush would feel delicious.
But in the tight demanding realm of
The conclusion of an idea, the hush
Would have to be the Seven Dwarfs, given Snow White
And the footprints of the Prince.

Given snow white and the footprints of the beavers
The hunter drew one conclusion across
The gleaming flat expanse . . . . .

Gasoline stains soak into your snow
Drained off into the pumps behind your back
Tall grass is waving you on. "I guess we better wipe
Our shields, scramble back into the seat
And push off."

DRIVING THROUGH BELGIUM

An old woman is cutting carnations
    and to them she seems like an old woman
Who cuts carnations: perfumes press to get her
    between the pages of *Poetry* magazine—

And because nothing interrupts her
    she cuts one too many, and heads of esteem for
Gentlefolk fall away in crumble sadness
    past the shifting potholes of our day

BIRTH PAINS

Something is holding your feet down bare and awash
in the fiberglass trinkets on the floor of the car.
It's not very difficult.
Periods . . . perhaps you don't even need periods
at the end of sentences unless sentences are cliffs.
You draw in the lines a delicate raw fish rises out of the sea

> "From the bottom of the sea
> A tasseled creature is nipped
> It cannot live beneath a tree
> Like you or me: it has to drip
> In order not to cry . . ."

Some city! It takes four hours
to walk to the car parked in your driveway—
maybe you should start from someplace
                    closer to home

Nostalgia, I started to go there

Please go to nostalgia passengers
Are requested to retain their CUSTOMS
DECLARATIONS in their pants and
Present them & TRAVEL DOCUMENTS to the
        IMMIGRATION OFFICER for stamping by hand

Happy children strain every muscle to remember
            and if they're happy enough, they do

So I was left with a choice: the suede
or the neige one. I chose the neige.

I chose the sage
and marjoram. You spilled the allspice.
He she it chewed the laurel.
We swooned under cinnamon. You chopped
the bay. They lay down in the mint.

They lay down in the mist
and, not to upset you, opened their eyes.
What they saw was very beautiful
and pleased you, it made you glad
and gave you hope to drink, like water . . .
No longer thirsty, no longer hunted
and afraid, you sat back in the little
cluster of pines, and laughed, and became an expert

Soon children, others too, they came to you
and asked you,   "Who are they
who lay down in the mist
and, not to upset you, opened their eyes?
What they saw was very beautiful
          although it destroyed T. S. Eliot"

Something is holding your trousers up
and obviously it's not the force of gravity.
You get up to see who's at the door
at this time of night

It's a night rider!
With a message, a telegram—
you are being called upon
        to form a new government
from among the following people:

> Miss Beatrice M. White
> Mrs. Florence G. Willan
> Mr. Frank Willekens
> Miss D. M. Willet
> Mr. Gene Williams
> Mrs. Williams
> Master Thomas Williams
> Mr. Forrest Wood
> Mrs. Wood
> Miss Cecile A. Wynter

CLEAN & CLEAR

At the little window is the tiny hand
At the big window is the giant hand
And both are open

A small opening but everyone is working
What is the worker doing? he is working
For light is the ensemble of the colors

The immense sun shines
At the window a tiny hand is drawing
No one on the street because his drawing is divan

One six blocks up
Six blocks to the corner, to the seven
The eight, the giant hand

Is filling the block with light
Six blocks in one corner
One giant in another

At the little window the tiny hand
Is no longer at the giant hand
The tiny hand is on the knob

LOUD POEM

Thank you   First what I'd like to do
Is read a small piece I received in mail

    Actually it's just a tiny piece
I broke off from the rest
    while you were sleeping
I put it into shallow water
    and it turns into a beautiful green fern
I change the water often to prevent it
    from becoming rancid

It's coming to life, now, before my very eyes
Although it's only a small part the other pieces
Are scattered all over, like the unfortunate body
Albertine Williams cut into three inch squares and mailed
To over ninety General Deliveries throughout the U.S.
    a chain reaction of grisly births
    before the trembling hands of disbelieving postmen

But this plant is a dry one
And appears dead and lifeless
        I just put it in a bowl of water
        And within 24 hours I have a nice
Fern   Later, if I wish, I may
        remove it and let it dry up
But return to water, and it will resurrect
        again & again
Because it is a piece of a "Resurrection Plant"

Because it is a piece of a "Resurrection Plant"
It is possible to lay dormant for 50 years
Yet spring to life when put again into water
As long as it was found free of dry-plant-destroying bacteria
And also originated in an area free from that
In accordance with the Nursery Inspection Laws of the
            State of Texas
Stock No. 134   Cactus Craft of Arizona   Tucson, Arizona

I'd like to finish by telling you
    exactly how this piece of plant came
to me, instead of to you, or to some postman

It was sent by a friend staying at the
    HEAD HOTEL
Steam Heated Modern Rooms with Bath and Phone
    "Where Many Find Relief from Asthma"
    Prescott, Arizona

"Dear Mike:

Last night I stayed at the above
Hotel on the square of Prescott—blue
White-tiled lobby, cowboys. I am
Writing this letter with my feet

Hanging into the Grand Canyon—a
Predawn smoke of hash the sun certainly
Coming up. There is something about
Groups of people standing on the starry

Edge of such a large event forced
To wait for the sun to rise.
    I met a fine 6-year-old head in Encinitas
And we blew many joints together

Watching the sun sink into the sea.
Acid continues to be a salvation as I
Am truly aloft as I slowly continue
East by way of the Navajo."

FINGERTIPS

Your translucent cousin appears underweight
And floats a little in the hand   that is
If you cross between it it glows
Mistaking the children for a walk
In far wood   still no noise
Pooped Mayans breaking for a silent loaf

Meal collapses, resting a bit behind in the hill
You descend to tell friends to "Park cars!"
For cold luncheon on the scarf
And park their cars until the lawn
And rub antler parked Mars
Friendly, although a single leaf
Grows from the thought and the way it grows
Someone on the lake hears the motor relax
And someone on the beach relaxes
Like a crowd of children who suppose

And then the old folk
Song, at the tip of your tongue:
"A dusky knee lines the pungent trees
Above and below the puffing crane
Aunt Lime deposits in her garden plans"

Wiping the grip from her shoulder
She rests, budging in the breeze
Over the warm population

Blue rustics in a sunny fog
Wobble a net of perfect summer
In fact, it is the sole net

POEM IN TWO PARTS

Pause before anything ordinary
            and it becomes important

SNOWBOUND

As this orange jockeys for position near my moving mouth
I forget that there's no longer a question of hunger
Even when I don't eat, or rather after I don't eat . . .
I tell myself mouthing the words absently
The story of the figure skater and the abandoned house
A story in name only as it actually occurred to the girl herself
To tell it to me shortly before she died engulfed
By what surrounded her, the victim of a fatal distance.
Her mouth was one of those things that make the old women
Hop and croak like frogs not on shore
When an outboard foams over them and they pass.

Or to put it another way at some point

In your life a determined odor say of chocolate
Takes over your nose and pries open your mouth
Even though you know it's not from the chocolate cigarettes
You've been smoking too much lately,
And forces you to take refuge on a porch step
And dream-meditate the chocolate mountains back in place
As an orange slowly gains the eastern summit.
It rests there, along with the sounding frogs
And other lakefront emanations, and the girl's remaining
Mouth, who was speaking to you from on her blades
Until the thaw set in and Spring
Began to blaze and drip.

THE FLEDGLING

I saw a fledgling rise up
Today and crack the book
Across his teacher's head who sat
A little further up the brook

That great man fell
Apart and to one side
His half-formed charge seized on
His shoes, and started in to stride

Then to gesticulate in master tones
Then to kneel, repair the book
And find a fledgling of his own
Until I rumbled, "Crook!"

Yes, until I "Rumbled!" crook.

JANICE

Janice fancies away from her tendon
River lifting off the eyes of the big politicians.
Politeness. A final erection
Of the great placid columns of the past.
Dog looks around: cat?

For as the green bow droops in the sky, squad cars hanging
Down to a pear. Adolf's tenderizer chants
Into an alley's sense of shoe

Supporting you. A brick (an extra leaf)
Rebuilds tension.   A baking brick,
Popularity in a certain nose at a certain point out.

FLOATING

A cloud was hidden by the sun as she steeped tea
drank under an opening in the window and stepped out
onto the lawn off the bare wood-plank porch. She wore old
red jersey over a hard happy body, and stared down
the slope before the house, a Japanese text and prints
under her left arm in the curve above her hip. A small flag
from the old Republic of China was her only ornament, and
it was sewn near the top of her jersey at about the collarbone.
She was a lover of Asian artifacts, cultures, and the varied
ways of life. But it was a serene, uncomplicated love, and
nothing much was needed to make her forget it. Releasing her
hold on these interests was like pushing over a Ming vase
filled with warm milk in a mound of dark summer topsoil.
The vase rolled a little and came to rest, blue and vermilion
porcelain part-designs showing through the green bunches
of leaves, with a touch of hot chocolate brown, the earth,
underneath. With her Hasselblad she would take a few color
slides of this release from preoccupation and, after they
were developed, project them onto one of the cool white plaster
walls inside her house. Whenever anyone asked me about her, I
would always say she lived "further down the road."

ZIP CODE

Six zebras galloping across
The middle distance

All but one of them
Glances at you

A sunny day, you have a red
Checked shirt and no jacket on

Now is the time, you feel
To photograph these animals

FROM THE JAPANESE

Someone has saki
Someone else has cups

They get together and yet
They remain apart:

Falling needle of the mountain pine

HIGHWAY TO THE SKY

A chair is growing in the woods
Where I left you searching for peace
That like a fine meal would make you whole again and ready
To spread your energy over chosen ground
And accept the fate of watching it grow

How slowly can you sit down?
Do you think you're able to stretch it over the time
While your shadow drifts and changes
And cosmos shows up around you
Lush, or even overwhelming?

Sit down, please. Check for sound. Light
A cigarette and visualize that somewhere
I'm lighting one too, and tender smoke
Tender because it disappears
Reaches the leaves on its way up.

AGAINST THE GRAIN

. . . either, over the shoulder enjoy leaning. Don't
Touch it. Skyway pumpkins lounge
Rocking beside me but I thrive straight
Away. Large early centers blur off   (Look, Johnny
See the Indians at home on their Maine blankets
Lobster smoke disappearing between the
Tree. Don't knock it over.)   looking over.

Would you turn it down a quarter inch?
Now I rest between the teeth of
Courage, silence, gold. I pass the lines
Painted below the pilot's "Otto" window
Like a lake going up from gasoline
To drowning above the clouds (of starch beauty).
Probing a border the police sighs
The trestle agh agh agh over the train late
Mathematics pass hot trees. Dutch door. Don't move.

I wander the banks and Wanda was.

Sounds not so much mingle curtains
Yellow against green and then of course
The perfect right green has against yellow
In the dusty white pod against here
Beside your wife who is too sinuous and tall
To be a real Dutch . . . little men in pocket charms
Made her. She travels . . . an easy window
Sunlight on Bavarian cottage window

In natural southern Bavaria. Large blue
Against the Pittsburgh sky. Sky.
Summer in the pedigree under Moscow's dome.

Take the summer.

She delivers a folded postcard to the hill.
Mingling feeds rain and forest an afterthought
As I am planning to feed astronomy
To the turkeys here for a year
(Light snows over the eighty mile ear)
Pure ground plum stew chugging up.

Early in the morning it quieted down somewhere
Among the flamingoes. Suddenly I realized this was because
They had no place to sit. I shaved for a while in the mirror
And crawling out of the tent (take the summer) I crawled
Out of the tent and talked over to the shore
Most of the people were eating already.

POUNDS AND OUNCES

Here comes Charles and Madeleina my child
India, Guerdon, Macao, Church and Bessarabia
A minute to the left of the knee
Louise, Esso, Essene and gold Dolores of the caves
To rest on views from the point
You begins to get up and leave   (pounce)

Yes, he should be blank in the parka by now
Most of the guests are, already receiving visits
You might walk over once more
Then he reads you out

Dirty and graceful but a bit too tall
Clean and distrustful but short little
Noreen and Barley are scrambling out of the Jumna to you
They think they are going to wave

"No Thought"

Egg   Spoon   Throat   Vista

Teeth   Glint   Spokes

Stagger   Choke

(Pearl)

Upon the pyramid I have returned to you
Ready to go. Dolores is folding her last slip in the mouth
"Pack clothes write batter and taste and see"
New spoons and fresh marching spoons
Baby Egypt damp with glee

DIAMOND

A heart speaks and you are spooked
Coming to rest upon Mt. Olympia
Instead of thirteen miles across noisy brown glare to Bridgeport
(in eastern U.S.)

And you rest your arms, a lemonade in blue glass
Soothes as if I soothe you
Like a factory in the night

Large factory: Lhasa toils gigantic
inside a cup you are drinking mountains
. . . a pork barrel hidden from
the gentle vegetarians digesting the sun . . .
flutes called up through gauze
of the Pink Brick Motel . . . freedman
caravans focus slowly over your clover bed . . .
clearing your throat you disturb another virgin lake

Small factory: rancid yak butter
cause you to laugh unawares as a testy goon
smites you in the rolling dawn of a particle . . .
gun slides on a far wall . . . piles
of bored newsmen in the corner
serve irritations begun as a closet
by taking up space . . . Pica
lettering the cat obscures

if you have a cat . . . I have a cat
I have a small ink eraser . . .
I have, here on the table as I write,
several dull books and the death of Stephen Crane

You shoot out of the lamination of a chair
To verify, not lists, but the sake of a list
In white porcelain cup, leaves

Of never having to carry your heart
Toward a storeroom that forces it to speak
Because actually you and I are always speaking

THE NEW REGIME

Today is the first day
Of the new regime
I hope to lose
Hundreds of pounds
And fear to lose
My personal freedom

As I look out
Over the popping sky
The new regime
Creases toward me
Zeros in

And from between my eyes
A tender dream is born
A flashlight's beam
Of righteous wariness
A lotus bloom of searing love

IN SEARCH OF THE MIRACULOUS

for Dick Gallup

Everything is very close together in the little town.
Houses, streets, and squares are all packed tight, ready
for instant removal. It's as if only a little jolt
were needed and everything would disappear again
through the zap.

Some who've been talking as they have entered these
villages have left them without saying a word.

Peace, please, to all the tilted heads.

This extraordinary act occurs unnoticed and un-
dramatically in the face. Therefore most human faces
appear calm.

We're human. We get just as big a wallop out of checkered
flags, silver cups, and champagne as the next guy. But when
we race we're not looking for applause: we're looking
for something else, I think.

I'd put on my blue overalls and head out to work dressed
like that, every day.

69

PUSHPALEELA

Soapy water swirls down the drain and I'm free,
the sunbeams flash across the floor, I open the morning
mail, plane crash, popcorn, no one left in jail. All this happens
during a single instant. How sweet it is, pushing off your
grey suede jacket and jackknifing for the pearl.

THE RAINBOW ROOM

O lovely lovely roast pork sandwich
and lovely blessed bottle of light brown
                    imported beer
and the general cool deliciousness of life:
I am ecstatic & I'm going to douse my forehead with
pitchers of "I see!" from the Rainbow Room

POCKET MANUAL

The astounding part of what you read to me
Starts the single engine on my star
Misty planet that likes regaining poise. But

Whether marksmen shatter the final cup
That filled the middle ear and, waking sound
To its supreme role as spear, or deeper than that
No man can tell: his talent is his hat
His handiwork the echo of a right hand:
The left, gladiola.   "I decorate myself for you"
He sings, but I sing too. I sing out. I revel
Not in tarnish although tarnish
Is a hunger anyone can feed, and right now
It's feeding a porpoise of chaos, but chaos
To compensate a tight-lipped order that sprays
From golden impudence across Space to you:

Hello? Yes, that's me. And you hang up as
The message describes its own phone, a red one
Bedside and silent near Pall Malls
On an end table. The table's varnished butt is flush
Against a cigarette burn on William
Morris tapestry covering the damp wall whose other side
Is part of southern English countryside, glowing
Under full moonlight as a plate.

                    And there are many more plates, for this
Is a luxury edition, I settle for it, it allows me
To flip three pages for example to Rangoon.
Volume I, NIGHT. Volume II, if you will kindly leave
The room to me, and when I discover a stretch of true
Leisure for art materials, DAY. A huge day
And soon we'll be bold enough
To eliminate the anachronism of a publisher.